# The Sea Shell Ship
## A Spiritual Poetry Collection

Dan T. Baldwin

The Sea Shell Ship

By Dan T. Baldwin

Copyright © 2024 Dan T. Baldwin

All rights reserved. No part of this book may be reproduced or transmitted in any form or by any means, electronic or mechanical, including photocopying, recording or by any information storage and retrieval system, without written permission from the author, except for the inclusion of brief quotations in a review.

First Edition 2024

ISBN 13: 978-1-952685-93-4

Edited by Reprospace, LLC
Cover Design by Reprospace, LLC

This is a work of fiction. Names, characters, places, and incidents either are the product of the author's imagination or are used fictitiously. Any resemblance to actual persons, living or dead, events, or locales is entirely coincidental.

The author has undertaken extensive research to provide an accurate depiction of the historical period and cultural practices. However, some elements have been fictionalized for narrative purposes. No disrespect or distortion of the actual history of Native American tribal life is intended.

Kitsap Publishing
Poulsbo, WA • USA

# DEDICATION

*To the dreamers, the seekers, and the quiet hearts—this collection is for those who find solace in solitude, wonder in the everyday, and magic in the unexpected. May these words be a refuge, a friend, and a spark in the darkness.*

# FOREWORD

### *by the Publisher*

It is my great privilege to introduce *The Sea Shell Ship* by Dan T. Baldwin, a profound collection that invites readers on a journey through the depths of the human experience. This work is not merely a book of poetry and prose; it is an intimate exploration of the joys, sorrows, and reflections that shape our lives. Each piece offers a unique glimpse into the heart of humanity, touching on themes of love, faith, sacrifice, and the quest for meaning.

Dan T. Baldwin's writing embodies an authentic voice, one that is unafraid to tackle both the beauty and the challenges of life. His words resonate deeply, drawing readers into a world that is both familiar and refreshingly new. Whether recounting the innocence of love, the horrors of war, or the solace found in nature, Baldwin's reflections evoke emotions that linger long after the final page is turned.

As a publisher, I am honored to bring this collection to you, our readers. It is a book that speaks to the soul, reminding us of the importance of introspection and the power of connection—with ourselves, with others, and with the world around us. I hope that "Sea Shell Ship" becomes a companion for you, offering solace, inspiration, and a renewed sense of wonder.

— Ingemar Anderson, Kitsap Publishing, Poulsbo, WA

# CONTENTS

Dedication
Foreword
THE STORY OF THE SEA SHELL SHIP i
A DECAT OF BEADS 1
A LETTER TO MOM 5
A LITTLE CHRISTMAS SPIRIT 7
A MANIFEST SOUL 9
A SIMPLE POEM 11
ALONE 13
AMONGST US 15
ANGELIC HYMS 17
ANOTHER DAY GONE 19
BEING LOVED 21
CAMELOT LOST 23
CONCERNED MISGIVINGS 25
EASTER 27
FANTASIES 29
FOUR ONCE MORE 31
GOD'S EYES 33
GOLF 35
ABOUT THE AUTHOR 39

# THE STORY OF THE SEA SHELL SHIP

By mid-1966, The U.S. Navy's 7th fleet was heavily committed to the Tonkin Gulf arena around Viet Nam. What started in 1965 as a purported defensive move against a Vietnamese patrol boat attacking a U.S. Navy destroyer had ballooned to over 385,000 troops plus over 60,000 U.S. sailors assigned to shore duty. The Subic Bay area in the Philippines was a hub of Navy R & R and ship resupply. Olongapo City at that time became an eye-opening experience for 18 to 25 year-old sailors with bars with young ladies, trinket ships, shoe shine boys on the street, and any number of open shops that seemed like an imitation of a gold rush town in a turn-of- the century Alaska. The most charming thing was called a *Jeepney*. A fleet of left over WWII jeeps converted to flamboyantly painted taxi's with Hispanic fringe balls tangling from every corner. The paint jobs on the jeeps would have made any graffiti painter in Los Angeles proud.

The 'four masted shea shell ship' which was created in Olongapo was made of a variety of sea shells including three sized sails mounted on each of the four masts. Luzon Island had been a Treassure trove of sea shells since the islands were first involved in trade. The collection of shells in itself was unique and 'ship in the bottle' bottle style art had dimensions of seven inches long and seven and one-half inches high. A letter from home had requested me to buy *'something'* from the Philippines for my fraternal grandmother. The sea shell ship was bought from one of the street shops on the main street while on shore leave on my second Subic Bay stop while overseas on my first West-Pac cruise. The small sea shell ship would become a life story thread which started when I was on active duty and last well into my seventies. I had mailed the ship home and put the matter out of my mind at the time of the letter request. My Grandmother passed away in 1972, just over three years after my discharge. The ship was passed along to an aunt that held the ship as a memory until the late-1980's. Out of sight, out of mind.

Earlier, In the late 1950's, my immediate family had moved to the Midway area of St. Paul, Minnesota. Our house was a large two-story built in the late 1880's. My bedroom had an oversized closet where my mother stored an old cedar chest with family pictures and some mementos of my father's time in Europe during WWII. One of these items was a picture of my father's younger brother Francis (Frankie) Baldwin that had given his life in Gen. Douglas MacArthur's retaking of the Philippine Islands. When I first found his picture in Army uniform, I had inquired who he was, since his name had not been mentioned. I found myself visiting the cedar chest due to some spiritual connection that I did not quite understand. I chose the name Francis as my Catholic Confirmation name in the 7th grade (St. Lukes Catholic School) in 1958. When one is 12 years old, it seemed a simple thought process. I was staying with my aunt Norene in the late 1980's and having an afternoon cocktail with her when she suddenly commented that she had something for me.

She went to the back of the house and reappeared to set the sea shell ship in front of me and said "this is yours." Clueless, I smiled at her with a question on my face. She noted it had been my Grandmother's. Still no clue, I politely said thankyou and accepted the gift as a memento of her.

The ship survived several moves from California to Washington to Arizona and back to the city of Redmond, Washington. And then two more pack and moves to different homes within Redmond. All without a chip or crack or broken sail. It was 2012 when I was re-arranging my home office shelving when I happened to use that old picture of Frankie from the cedar chest and placed it on a shelf next to the sea shell ship along with a picture of my father, now also deceased. The light went on! Along the way, I had been doing some genealogy work when I discovered that Frankie had actually been buried in a military cemetery in Olongapo and related the ship to the letter request for a memento from my mother.

By this time, I had also collected Frankie's 'Killed in Action notice' from the St. Paul Pioneer Press. Later, I discovered that the cemetery in Olongapo had been relocated to a more formal military cemetery in Manila. The ship became a thread in my other genealogy stories and re-ignited that spiritual connection from my grade school Confirmation.

In the 2021-2022 period of the Covid lockdown, my impulse to collect my past periodic poetry from the late 1970's to 2010 became focused and I added thirty-five new poems to the collection. I stopped to count the collection one day and discovered almost fifty poems. The writings had been more the result of inspiration than a work in progress. I searched for a name of the work, noting that it was 50 poems from Viet Nam to Covid, but found myself staring at the ship, still on a shelf after the last relocation to a 55+ retirement community. The Sea Shell Ship which had now survived over 50 years in my care and just seemed to talk to me. Coincidence, impulse, and the sense that much of my life was filled with stories like the ship were actually threads in a life tapestry.

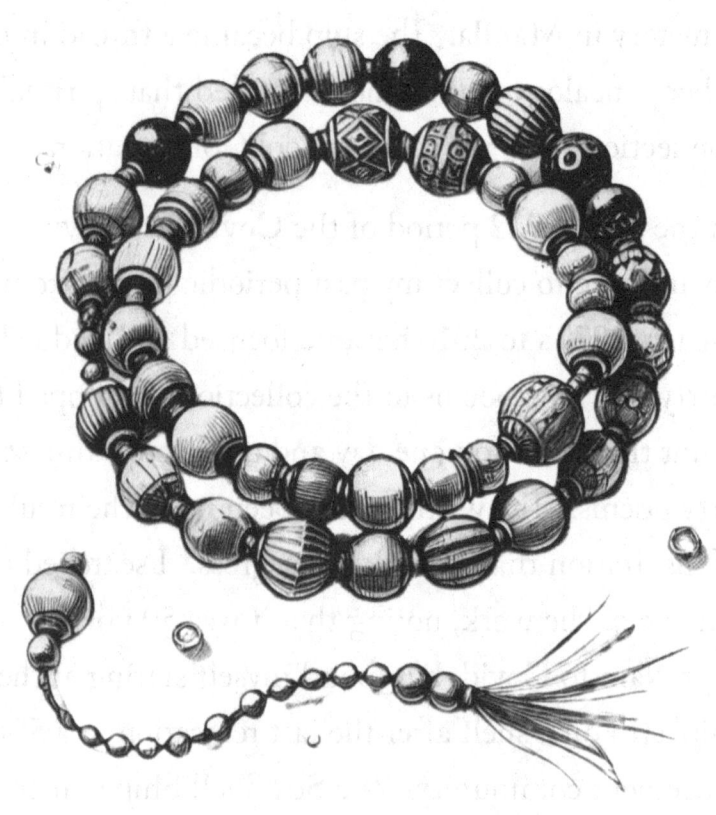

# A DECAT OF BEADS

Before being borne to a wealthy family a virgin child was avowed to live in a temple that protected a holy ark encasing the ten rules of virtue, she, a descendant of the fruit of the Tree of Jesse with a heritage of kings as scripture had foretold was to become the mother of all human beings.

Then as a maid already with child, she was betrothed from that temple, destined to become the mother of a king on the day the earth stood still and as her child was borne under an angelic star in mankind's straw cradle, she suckled that child with seven spirits born to become earth's Paraclete.

In the child's first year a priestly philosopher forecast to her that this child would become the sword that would pierce this blessed mother's very heart, a wound allayed by angelic encounters to give her the calm to play her part that would only unfold thirty years later as divine prophesies had foretold.

That child was destined to be publicly tested, humbled, and tortured as few men have ever been, then nailed, roped, and hung there on a cross limb tree as his mother watched, she shed wretched tears of blood as He suffered for for all mankind and the sword foretold pierced her heart in burning anguish.

This comforting mother has oft revisited this earth to tell us of a heavenly grace, of a circular metal rope, a string of life set in five meditative decats that pace like a chant, a simple prayer, an intimacy, to allay this world's most base fears and provide us with an intimacy with that mother and child in a humble Rosary.

As faith begets hope, Religion should not be a wall to keep all the wanderers from a simple truth offering.

# A LETTER TO MOM

*Brought home by Thomas F. Baldwin from the Battle of the Bulge—Author Unknown*

I'm down in a hole made by a shell
The guns around me are making it hell.
With the flash of a gun I can see a lad
Who should be home with his Mom and Dad.

By the flash of another I can see his face
It's white and drawn as if made of paste.
He's coming my way now. It's he or I
neither one of us want to die.

I shot him Mom. He fell with a scream
this war is worse than my craziest dream.
I'm praying to God to give me strength
through this terrible war that has no length.

He was a good-looking boy. About twenty-one
It was I who killed him! Lord. The harm being done.
I was trained to do so, there's a war to be won.

# A LITTLE CHRISTMAS SPIRIT

We have a list of people we know all written in a book
And every year at Christmas time, we go and take a look.

And that is when realize that those names are a part not of the book they're written in, but of the very heart.

So, when we send a Christmas card that is addressed to you it is because you're on that list of friends that we hold dear and true.

And whether we have known you for many years or few, you've been a hear felt part in shaping the lives and things we do.

This, the spirit of Christmas that is forever and ever endures may it leave its richest blessing, HOPE, in the hearts of you and yours.

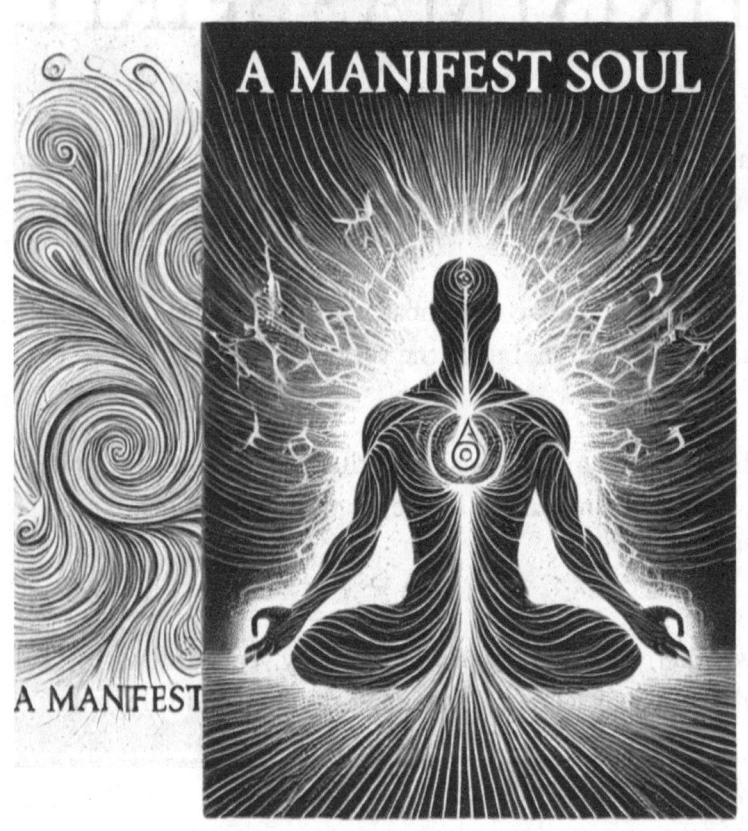

# A MANIFEST SOUL

How is it that they appear and seem to come and go and
reappear at periodic times every few years or so
A kindly act seemingly at random or just simple smile
To brighten a day, a moment, without a sign of guile

To lift a moment of life, a tiring, perhaps dreary day
with the twinkle in their eyes as they pass by my way
and lighten the cross or burden that I may bear
some fear disappears knowing a stranger may care

Should have said hello or perhaps good day to you
to bolster a lonely soul that just reached out too
could it have been a twinkle or a tear I'd seen
coming from the heart of a lost human being

As I turn over in my sleep, can their prayers be the same
under the burden of a cross just given a different name
I know next time that I shall wish that person a God Bless
for a soul that touched mine in that moment manifest.

# a simple poem

# A SIMPLE POEM

We have more temptations to become good versus bad is a start since everything that happens in the world happens first in the heart so wars originate and rise from thousands of individuals with ego needs the selfishness and pride that burn inside for honor from public deeds.

Accused of suffering from the sin and blindness of injustice and intolerance.

By those who veil their manipulations with the virtue of a broadminded stance and embarked on a ship claiming a great task as they began their journey without acknowledging the goals plan or who would be left mourning.

A new truth, and old truth, a simple truth, all seem so easy to find but it should not be invented, nurtured just for favor, to follow in a blind until our conscience bothers us and gives birth to a black misery inside that may be remembered as the children who died and a parent who cried.

The volumes of noise and words from people that seem unhappy inside emanate from an empty life and pace with no point or virtue, only pride looking for something outside you when it truly is buried inside your heart found on a bended knee seeking the essential ingredients to the omission part.

# ALONE

# ALONE

Go Wander upon this rotating rock for that place of solace
within a forest or upon a hill with a fiery golden sunset glow
that is sought to settle a restless mind that God should know
but did not send forth an answer to that prayer of wonder.
It happens when His house no longer sustains a soul and the
spiritual side of life becomes the goal answering the quest
to resolve that pain of loneliness to quench that awful thirst
for an audience before the soul or the heart should burst.

First distress then anger comes to meet some empty cries
of being abandoned in that place filled with hopeless sighs
where can that cup of hope be found to fill that empty soul
and find a little sustenance to place in a bottomless bowl.

Where then does such an answer lie to replace the sorrow of
loneliness and abandonment and appease a need to be content
need only to look behind when you walked away in indifference
from that moment when you needed to forgive and then repent.

# AMONGST US

There are many men amongst us who are individually good and share themselves and their children as any man should but too few are united together in a body, loving one another like organs in a body, a spiritual body, unlike any living other.

A player in a melodic orchestra, what humanity was meant to be not trapped in time from past to future at the expense of Christianity the theologians, the philosophers, and scientists, setting the precedence as life becomes moment by moment, we then see life like a sentence.

What we seem to be missing in life is the enigmatic spiritual touch of soul.

While leaders invent morality of the individual, and fairness as the goal  then man versus man, and power takes hold, Christian versus non-Christian resolved in war and greater power, the old sense of temperance seems a sin.

# ANGELIC HYMS

There is a secret in the Bible known as the Book of Joy
The first chapter which is made of mirth and song
of angels' chorus of joyous lyrics, hymns, and carols
that ring the heavenly sprits and fill the empty souls.

The pages in this book are not numbered to count
But when you flip the pages, there appears a font
of color with white doves raising their wings in praise
to fly in a rainbow that reaches from earth to azure.

The Holy Spirit writes the verse, melody, and lyrics
then conducts the celestial voices in many chorales
so all you have to do to listen is just close your eyes
and hear the wind in the sublime disguise of paradise.

Take Joy in this world for the gifts you've been given
And try to listen to that Joy on this side of heaven
when a short personal prayer, such a simple request
is to be worthy of the sacrifices another has given.

# ANOTHER DAY GONE
### A POEM

# ANOTHER DAY GONE

Another day goes drifting by as I watch a small sparrow duck and dive while a warm wind flattens and stretches the silky clouds sailing by and one by one they flatten out one upon the other like a layer cake and purple light glows between the layers while the sun dances on a lake in a haze while the young sparrow flitters off into the sunset as light is lost, daylight dies, and a pastel palate overcomes so only stars are left to twinkle.

Like a passage of a friend, that light again slipped by the mountains shadow while the dark blue of the lake casts shadows of shimmering friendships that only death can rob and seems not to care a slip for that comrades worth since death has no friends nor even a prayer to call his own, only a curse upon that curtain that comes to cover that last color hewed striated sky leaving a glow of memories, mirth, and bonded destiny, as it claims a friend.

# BEING LOVED

IF SOMEBODY LOVES YOU,
YOU CANNOT BE SAD.

YOU'VE CAUSE FOR REJOICING, CAUSE TO BE
GLAD YOU'VE A SUBJECT FOR A SONG, AS YOU
GO YOUR WAY IF SOMEBODY LOVES YOU, YOUR
HEART SHOULD BE GAY FOR LOVE, AFTERALL,
IS THE PURPOSE OF LIFE, THE PURPOSE OF
STRUGGLE, TURMOIL, AND STRIFE;

IF SOMEBODY LOVES YOU,
WHY WORRY AND SIGH?

IT'S FOR LOVE WE ARE LIVING,
AND LOVE DOES NOT DIE.

# CAMELOT LOST

They were quieter times with no autos moving on the avenues and the noises of children's voices were absent from the streets, most stores were closed and men still observed a sabbath day as Dad would read the Sunday paper by the large window bay.

Parking lots were filled at almost every denominations temple, church, synagogue, or mosque by faithful disciples seeking a prayerful search of finding liberty and hope while freeing themselves from a schism becoming a domination and bondage of man in a land of endless vision.

Then a President was murdered and America entered a Ten-Year War English bands became a new religion as society was changed at its core And if one entered military service then, he returned as youth was torn Replaced by a military industrial complex that infiltrated like a time worm

As sports and games liberalized families' time we began to forfeit inner liberty while embroiled in a realm of time which fostered something bitter as we abandoned Sundays like an imposition upon efficient working time enhanced by Daylight Saving Time, fluoride in the water, all seemed not a crime.

The party lines and rotary phones that disappeared with advances in digita impositions that dismissed neighbors talking over fences, we grew small as we passed by the advent of credit cards, with trips to the moon and Mars as America left that gentler time of a Camelot's sabbath for something too far.

# CONCERNED MISGIVINGS

Have the voices lashed out in your mind before
like titanic waves against a rocky boulder'd shore
till the sound causes you to writhe in some agony
and painfully are almost brought to your knees

So the angry voices in me have steadily grown
and pleaded my innermost secrets to be known
or perhaps my own pretenses could deceive
the emotions that a simple heart would believe

Hence, I exist in a longing and sorrowful way
afraid to ask or tell and to embarrassed to say
or ask a stranger if another has felt this way before
and I keep waiting another day and then a little more.

# Easter

A POEM SKETCH

# EASTER

Dear Lord, we cannot always rely on our own strength,

so bless us that we may be open to receive your help:

Bless our minds that we may meditate on your mysteries:

Bless our ears that we may hear your voice:

Bless our lips that we may always honor your love:

Bless our hearts that we might know your love; and

The Jelly Bean Prayer

RED is for the blood you sacrificed

YELLOW is for the brightness of the sun

WHITE is for a new life begun

GREEN is for the grass and trees

ORANGE is for the evenings glowing breeze

PINK is for the mornings first light

And on this EASTER, we pray in your name.

# FANTASIES

Fantasies are those personal little private memories
Hidden in sight from the world like foundling trees
Blossoming in the world at large but never shared
perhaps the exception being the person it faired.

A delightful moment, and oblivious escape from time
meant to create a smile and let a streak of light shine
as a brief lapse from some daily worry or troubles
seasoned with calm and just a glimmer of ecstasy.

Placed in a sliver locket for future safe keeping
a secret thought kept there and continues shining
placed before the world and kept so near one's heart
a place near the beginning of that fantasies start.

# Four Once More

# FOUR ONCE MORE

As I ambled down a cemented path, I stared into a tunnel of aged chestnut trees that were line up like old sentinels for over an endless shadowy mile.

The bright blue sky peeked through like wispy darts of willowy breezes, morning sun, and waves of delight being imparted by long limbed trees.

So enchanted by the site I walked with hands in pockets, head held high I wandered off the path following my soul until I bumped my head so hard against an old light pole.

# GOD'S EYES

A pink sky set against a blue misty morning hue
Venus in the East shining against a full moon
beauty that defies that the prophesied end is soon
but one can believe that God's teary eyes are blue.

Fear not those who manifest to deprive a body of life
they can only take the flesh of the dimpled flesh of babes
they do not command the soul of the helpless bairn
and their own souls will bear an endless Gehenna strife.

God sees the lawyers who build tombs for these innocents.
And deplore their bane who have murdered these children
so they may lose or gain in the joy and pain my youthful friend
but you must know that your own soul is your conscience.

# GOLF

Those seasoned friends from social clubs, sports, work and life who know your score of jokes and about your kids and your wife who've shared some hardships, hopes, and dreams and a little strife.

They became a resource in foursomes to compete on a softer scale.

A measure of whom you trust when you may win or perhaps fail but offer no sympathy when you when you simply miss a shot the gain or loss is a contest of pride, the price, a quarter in the pot.

# Editorial Commentary

"Sea Shell Ship" is a journey—a voyage through the emotions and stories that make us human. Written by Dan T. Baldwin, this collection brings together poetry and prose that seek to connect with the reader on a deeply personal level. It is a book that aims to bring to light both the triumphs and trials of the human experience, capturing moments that are at once ephemeral yet enduring in our hearts and minds.

Each piece in this collection holds a mirror to different facets of life. Some pages may speak of love and longing, while others recount the poignant weight of loss or the quiet joy found in a fleeting moment of beauty. Baldwin's words invite you to reflect, to imagine, and perhaps even to heal. There is a certain intimacy in the way the author weaves together narrative and verse, one that reminds us that, at our core, we share many of the same hopes, fears, and desires.

"Sea Shell Ship" is also a tribute to resilience—the resilience of the human spirit as it encounters love, faith, loneliness, and even the challenges of modern life. By offering a candid portrayal of the struggles and triumphs that shape us, Baldwin crafts an honest and empathetic view of what it means to be alive. The stories and poems in this collection are not only meant to be read but to be felt, to encourage us to think more deeply about our own experiences and how they relate to those around us.

It is my hope that, as you read this book, you will find moments that resonate with your own journey. Let this collection serve as a reminder that we are never truly alone—that there are always words, thoughts, and experiences that can connect us across time and space. May "Sea Shell Ship" be a source of inspiration and reflection, a book that you return to whenever you need to find solace, meaning, or simply the beauty in life's small moments.

# ABOUT THE AUTHOR

Dan T. Baldwin

My poetic story started while doing two tours of Vietnam while in the Navy from 1965 to 1969. Simple poetic lines were typed and then dumped in an 8 ½ x 11 folder and stuffed in a drawer.

## ABOUT THE AUTHOR

In the late 1970s, while finishing a B.A. degree, a series of acquaintances, including a college professor, a Harvard-trained psychiatrist who happened to be a Catholic priest and a personal friend, each casually mentioned that I had a unique look at the world and a writing ability. These friendly suggestions were mentally placed in that same 8 ½ x 11 folder and stuffed back in the drawer. After retiring from 40 years of corporate life in 2010, I did have a somewhat full folder and decided to look at the creative side of life. Creativity is a tough, questionable skill.

The ability to treat writing as a daily mental and physical commitment created new challenges and focus points. I began to organize the poems and random observations from that old folder. Then, when COVID broke in the USA and America was locked away, I found time to concentrate on my poetic thoughts and experiences. Rhymes, simple limericks, or actual poetry were rolling around in my head like a merry-go-round, and I felt the compulsion to organize. So, a limerick is a simple poem put into four or five lines, followed by two more lines offering a humorous closing. A poem normally focuses on sentiment, the content of feelings, and even a simple expression such as passion, which has similar sounding words used at the end of the line. Rhyming words used in a poem do not seem to be compulsory. A poem may use rhyming words in a pattern, but they don't need to rhyme at the end of a line.

The old expression about the glass of water being half full or half empty becomes meaningless when one views the world looking up through the bottom of the glass with an Irish point of view. I have tried to include the sentiment of the *Sea Shell Ship* story in four categories. They are a collection of life experiences and disappointments that evolved into a poetic release.

www.ingramcontent.com/pod-product-compliance
Lightning Source LLC
Chambersburg PA
CBHW011407070526
44586CB00022B/2594